# SWING HIGH

Life Lessons from Childhood

Anthony Gunn

# Swing High

## Life Lessons from Childhood

hardie grant books

MELBOURNE · LONDON

*To my two beautiful children,*
*Emma and Patrick, who have pushed me out*
*of many comfort zones by teaching me the*
*importance of being a child again.*

# 1. Push yourself

When a child uses a swing they'll often try and go as high as they can. As adults we seem to lose this ability to push ourselves and instead prefer to play it safe. Push yourself to swing high and success will follow, disproving anyone who said you couldn't achieve.

*'Success is the most satisfying and legal form of revenge.'*
— CHRIS HARDWICK

# 2. Avoid the Goldilocks complex

Goldilocks was a total perfectionist, always wanting things to be just right. But rarely is anything in life just as we want it. Unlike adults, children are usually happy with less than perfect. Instead of always aiming for 100 per cent in your life, try aiming for 80 per cent. You'll get a lot more done and feel happier for it.

> *'Have no fear of perfection –*
> *you'll never reach it.'*
> – SALVADOR DALI

# 3. Trophy-up your fridge

Children are masters of acknowledging their achievements, they always want to put their paintings or awards on the fridge. Make a habit of acknowledging your achievements. Even better, make a list of them and put it on the fridge. In time, this will be a great motivator to keep achieving.

*'My most brilliant achievement was my ability to be able to persuade my wife to marry me.'*
– WINSTON CHURCHILL

# 4. Use fear to your advantage

Fear of the dark starts at about three years of age, the time when a child's brain develops imagination. Children are brilliant at coming up with really scary scenarios. If you have a fear, try coming up with a bigger fear. If you're anxious about going to the gym, then imagine the possible health problems that could arise from not going. Try it and see.

*'Monsters are real, and ghosts are real too.*
*They live inside us, and sometimes, they win.'*
— STEPHEN KING

# 5. Love your birthday candles

Children love blowing out their birthday candles. They'll boast about their age to anyone who'll listen. Unlike adults in western culture who fear getting old, eastern cultures see ageing like children do – as an achievement. Ageing is part of life. Go with it instead of fighting it. It's less work that way and may even help you look younger.

*'Ageing can be fun if you lay back and enjoy it.'*
— Clint Eastwood

# 6. Be childish when it comes to struggle

Have you ever tried helping a child who was struggling to tie their shoelaces or butter their toast, only to have them forcefully tell you to back off? Children will often keep going until they master a task, whereas as adults we can give up before we've even really started. Struggle like a child.

*'Consider the postage stamp: its usefulness consists in the ability to stick to one thing till it gets there.'*
— Josh Billings

# 7. Listen with your eyes

At birth, a baby's eyes are nearly the same size as an adult's. This is why babies look so cute – their eyes are out of proportion to the size of their head. Children use their large eyes to advantage by fully observing their surroundings. Go for a walk and focus on what you can see instead of thinking where you have to be. It's a great way for your mind to unwind.

*'You can observe a lot by just watching.'*
– Yogi Berra

# 8. Try not to compare

A common way that adults inflate their self-esteem is by comparing ourselves to those who are worse off. The problem is that these good feelings don't last long, so we have to keep on making comparisons and putting more and more people down. Children, on the other hand, enhance their self-esteem by bettering themselves and reaching personal goals. Go on, set a personal goal and see if you can achieve it.

*'Women are so unforgiving of themselves.*
*We don't recognise our own beauty because we're*
*too busy comparing ourselves to other people.'*
— KELLY OSBOURNE

# 9. Ditch your drama addiction

Have you ever bought a magazine or watched a TV show just to get a fix of celebrity drama? Ever noticed that children aren't interested in this kind of sensation? Why? Because children's lives are rarely dull. They're constantly exploring and trying new things. Give the celebrity gossip a rest and go explore your surroundings instead.

*'Drama is life with the dull bits cut out.'*
– ALFRED HITCHCOCK

# 10. Avoid the shoe blues

If you were like many children, you probably wouldn't have liked wearing shoes very much when you were young. Get back in touch with nature, and your senses, by walking barefoot on grass, sand or in water. Notice how it feels: it's guaranteed to put a smile on your face.

*'Heaven is under our feet*
*as well as over our heads.'*
– HENRY DAVID THOREAU

# 11. Make reading like breathing

Bedtime stories are a hit with kids. Just try putting a child to bed without their usual story and see what happens. Reading acts not only as an escape but is also a great tool to better ourselves. Commit to reading daily.

*'The man who does not read good books has no advantage over the man who cannot read.'*
– MARK TWAIN

# 12. Nag off rejection

Children have a natural ability to never accept 'no' for an answer. They'll keep asking until they get what they want. But as adults we somehow lose this persistence and instead we don't speak up for fear of being told no. What is it in life you want? Imagine if you were a child and wouldn't take no for an answer. What could you achieve?

*'It's not that I'm so smart,*
*it's just that I stay with problems longer.'*
– ALBERT EINSTEIN

# 13. Try going out of the lines

A child learning to colour-in will often go out of the lines and yet still be proud of their work. Fearing rejection from others can cause us to conform and stay within the lines of society. Step out of your self-imposed lines and take three small risks. Feeling wrong will never feel so right.

*'There's something liberating about not pretending. Dare to embarrass yourself. Risk.'*
— DREW BARRYMORE

# 14. Make mud pies

Children can see beauty in things adults often miss. The pride children take in making a mud pie is amazing. A lump of muck, once worked, transforms into gold. Try it. Pick up some shapeless, dirty old mud and shape it into something. From then on you'll see mud differently. What other things in life are you missing the beauty of?

*'Everything has its beauty,*
*but not everyone sees it.'*
— CONFUCIUS

# 15. Believe again

What did you want to be when you were a child? Maybe an astronaut, superhero or a vet? The belief children have in themselves is astounding. Your self-belief from childhood is still there, but long denied. What's that idea you've wanted to follow up on but haven't? Try ignoring the 'what ifs' and take action.

> *'Difficult things take a long time,*
> *impossible things a little longer.'*
> – ANDRÉ A. JACKSON

# 16. Talk to a teddy bear

As a child, did you talk to your teddy bear or toys? Research shows that when we talk about a problem instead of mulling over it in our mind, we use a different part of our brain. That's why we can often solve our own issues as we're talking about them. If you can't talk to a friend, try talking to your pet, God, the ocean or the sky. Just get those problems out.

*'In a world gone bad, a bear – even a bear standing on its head – is a comforting, uncomplicated, dependable hunk of sanity.'*
— PAM BROWN

# 17. Hold your tongue

Do you have trouble controlling your anger?
Try this one. Next time you're angry, say
what you want but there's one catch – you
must hold your tongue with your fingers as
you speak. Children laugh when they try this
challenge. Tap into your inner child and see
if you can still remain angry.

*'Anger is just anger. It isn't good. It isn't bad.
It just is. What you do with it is what matters.
It's like anything else. You can use it to build
or to destroy. You just have to make the choice.'*
– JIM BUTCHER

# 18. Manage impressions like a kid

Have you ever considered that the reason we iron our clothes might be because we're worried what others think of us? Psychologists call this impression management. Ever notice how children are often oblivious to other people's opinions of them? What would your life be like if you were less worried about keeping up appearances?

*'I can't give you a sure-fire formula for success,*
*but I can give you a formula for failure:*
*try to please everybody all the time.'*
— HERBERT BAYARD SWOPE

# 19. Ask why

Children often ask the question 'Why?'.
Why is the sky blue? Why do catfish have
whiskers? Why can't dads have babies? As
adults we lose this ability to question for fear
of what others will think of us. However, in
asking questions, growth occurs. Be like a
child and ask 'Why?' more often.

> *'A wise man can learn more from*
> *a foolish question than a fool can*
> *learn from a wise answer.'*
> – BRUCE LEE

# 20. Put the 'U' back in delusion

Kids are great at thinking they're better than they are. Adults are excellent at thinking we're worse than we are. Try this experiment: take on some child-like confidence and do something you've never done before – something you're sure you'll fail at. You may feel at first that it's a little delusional, but you might just prove yourself wrong.

*'Confidence is 10 per cent hard work and 90 per cent delusion.'*
    – TINA FEY

# 21. Don't be fooled by greed

Show a young child two rows of lollies: one where four lollies are spread out in a line, and the other row where six lollies are bunched up in a shorter line. Chances are they'll choose the longer looking row of four, thinking it has more in it. It's easy for us to see how greed clouds a child's judgement, but is buying things you can't afford on credit much different? How is greed distorting your life?

*'The greatest discovery of my generation is that human beings can alter their lives by altering their attitudes of mind.'*
— WILLIAM JAMES

# 22. Tap into your artistic streak

Everyone needs a break from the pressures of everyday life, and holidays aren't always possible. Instead of getting away, get back to your childhood and try being creative by doing art. Forget the excuse that you're not artistic. Just focus on the process and you'll bust that myth about yourself.

> *'Art is the only way to run away*
> *without leaving home.'*
> – TWYLA THARP

# 23. Contact your friends

For many children, going past their friend's house without dropping in to say hello is near impossible. Why? Because children love to make contact with their friends. Go on, contact that friend you've been putting off. You'll feel great for it.

*'It's sad when friends become enemies, but what's even worse is when they become strangers.'*
— HAYLEY WILLIAMS

# 24. Ask yourself, 'What would a child do?'

A tall truck was stuck in a low tunnel. Workmen were discussing whether to dismantle the truck's roof or the tunnel's ceiling when a child said, 'Why not let the air out of the tyres?' Adults complicate things; children see things simply. When faced with a problem, ask, 'What would a child do?'

*'You cannot look in a new direction by looking harder in the same direction.'*
— Edward de Bono

# 25. Are you the fun police?

Do you find that you're often too serious and scared to open up? Unlike adults, children are serious about not being serious. Their goal is to have fun. What can you do, starting today, to let down your guard and have fun? It's time to hang up your Fun Police badge.

*'People rarely succeed unless they have fun in what they are doing.'*
— DALE CARNEGIE

# 26. Have a crazy week

Life is serious – just ask any adult. We take ourselves very seriously. Kids are great at laughing at themselves, especially when they do something crazy. Here's a challenge. For the next week do something crazy each day. It could be skipping in public, whistling in a crowded elevator or using an unusual voice to order food at the drive-through. Go on, do something crazy, even for a short moment, and break the seriousness routine.

> *'Taking crazy things seriously*
> *is a serious waste of time.'*
> – HARUKI MURAKAMI

# 27. Don't let up

Children know what they want, whether it's a toy, a treat, the blue cup as opposed to the red cup, or their toast buttered on the other side. A child won't let up until they get what they want. Let your inner child speak up and become single-minded toward your life goal.

*'If you want nothing, do what you want.*
*If you want everything, develop discipline.'*
— KOSTYA TSZYU

# 28. Avoid bragging

Do you remember the kids at school who would always brag about how good they were? They weren't often kids who had very many friends. It's important to acknowledge your achievements, but don't throw them in other people's faces. Let people discover your strengths through your actions, not your words.

> *'Tell me what you brag about*
> *and I'll tell you what you lack.'*
> — SPANISH PROVERB

# 29. Mind your own business

Children rarely, if ever, partake in gossiping about others. We adults, on the other hand, often love gossiping and feeding off other's misfortunes because it makes us feel more adequate. The problem is that gossiping doesn't amount to anything and encourages other people to gossip about you. Next time someone tempts you to gossip about another person, hold your tongue.

*'If you read someone else's diary,*
*you get what you deserve.'*
– DAVID SEDARIS

# 30. *Satisfice*, don't optimise!

*Satisficing* is settling for the first solution that will do. *Optimising* is endlessly looking for a better solution. When choosing between everyday things, like when you're buying shoes, optimising causes indecision. Children are satisficers; they like an instant result. For routine things, be like a child by making a quick decision and accepting it.

*'Happiness can exist only in acceptance.'*
– GEORGE ORWELL

# 31. Bust the myth of multi-tasking

Have you ever seen a child multi-tasking? It's unlikely. Instead they need to concentrate on one thing at a time if they want to do it well. Multi-tasking is simply rapidly redirecting our attention between different tasks. Multi-task and you're not giving your full attention to the job at hand. For important tasks, act like a child and focus on one thing at a time.

*'You can do anything, but not everything.'*
– DAVID ALLEN

# 32. See yourself through a child's eyes

A teacher asks a child what their daddy does. The child answers, 'Walks around the house a lot, he's in charge sometimes and plays his computer.' Remove your rose-coloured glasses, take your ego down a few notches and avoid the pitfalls of vanity by imagining how your behaviour looks through a child's eyes.

> *'The knowledge of yourself will preserve you from vanity.'*
> — MIGUEL DE CERVANTES

# 33. Thrice your fear

Children learn best through games. Adults are no different. Here's a challenging game for you. Choose a small challenge you've been putting off facing and face it on three separate occasions. After that you will have gained the ability to choose whether or not you face that fear again.

*'Try a thing you haven't done three times.*
*Once, to get over the fear of doing it. Twice, to*
*learn how to do it. And a third time, to figure*
*out whether you like it or not.'*
– Virgil Garnett Thomson

# 34. Find a role model

Children love having a role model to look up to. Whether it's a superhero, famous performer or athlete, children gain inspiration and motivation to excel from their heroes. We learn by watching others and watching successful people helps teach success. Who's your role model, and are they a positive one?

*'I remember a specific moment, watching my grandmother hang the clothes on the line, and her saying to me, "you are going to have to learn to do this," and me being in that space of awareness and knowing that my life would not be the same as my grandmother's life.'*
– OPRAH WINFREY

# 35. Love someone perfectly

Children are often very accepting of others' differences. Yet in our adult relationships, the biggest threat to the relationship is often seeing the person as defective because they're not more like us. You are a one-of-a-kind, so finding someone just like you is going to be impossible. Instead, learn to see the positives in a relationship without comparing the other person to you.

*'We come to love not by finding a perfect person, but by learning to see an imperfect person perfectly.'*
— SAM KEEN

# 36. Make the calendar your friend

Christmas, birthdays, holidays and being invited to a friend's party are examples of things that keep a child in suspense. It's a great feeling counting down the time to an exciting event in the future. What's more, this positive feeling is contagious and will seep into other areas of your life. What can you do to look forward to something in the near future?

*'No matter how old you are, there's always something good to look forward to.'*
– LYNN JOHNSTON

# 37. Know your toaster

Most adults take modern technology for granted, while children often want to know how things work. Choose one household item and imagine you have to explain its workings to a child. Research your item on the internet to find out how it works. Doing so will open your mind to new ways of thinking. Researching your toaster is a fascinating place to start. Try it!

*'We live in a society exquisitely dependent on science and technology, in which hardly anyone knows anything about science and technology.'*
— CARL SAGAN

# 38. Play *spotto*

My children love playing a game called *spotto*, where the first person to call out 'spotto' when they see a yellow car gets a point. The champion is the person who spots the most yellow cars. Playing spotto will open your eyes to other things in the environment you've never noticed. Your challenge is to spot at least five yellow cars before the week is over.

> *'Raising awareness on the most pressing environmental issues of our time is more important than ever.'*
> – Leonardo DiCaprio

# 39. Conduct a bling assessment

When my son was little he lost his teddy bear. We tried offering him other things from his toy chest, but he wasn't interested. All the toys and bling meant nothing. In a time of crisis, how much of the 'bling' in your life would you actually want or need?

*'It's not having what you want,
it's wanting what you've got.'*
— SHERYL CROW

# 40. Pack away the crystal ball

Adults don't take children's predictions all that seriously. Whether it's being attacked by the monster under the bed or no-one liking them at school, we usually laugh them off. However, if an adult predicts the worst, especially if it's an economy expert on TV, we panic. People of all ages are terrible at predicting the worst. You've been warned!

> *'Prediction is very difficult,*
> *especially about the future.'*
> – Niels Bohr

# 41. Think before you buy

Often children have more fun with a large cardboard box than an expensive toy because playing with the box allows them to use their imagination. Adults buy things we think we need, but our imagination is only engaged when we're shopping for the item and not once we have it. Next time you're walking around a shop, ask yourself how you'll feel once you've purchased the item you're dreaming about.

*'The richest man is not he who has the most, but he who needs the least.'*
– Author Unknown

# 42. Rethinking death

Death can be a difficult topic to explain to children. Why? Because sometimes adults are terrified of even talking about death for fear that talking about it might make it come true. This is called magical thinking. Just thinking something won't make it come true. If it did we'd all be lottery winners. Death at some point is certain. How you live your life until then isn't.

> *'Don't be afraid of death so much*
> *as an inadequate life.'*
> – BERTOLT BRECHT

# 43. Do it yourself

Children are very self-sufficient when they have to be. If you need a spaceship built, give a child a large cardboard box, coloured paper, sticky tape and a marker, and leave them to it. Adults often lose this self-sufficiency for fear of making a mistake. This causes a dependence on others. Try having a go at doing something that you would normally ask someone else to do.

*'Chop your own wood,*
*and it will warm you twice.'*
— HENRY FORD

# 44. Treat yourself to an improved you

It's been said that children have two speeds, flat-out and asleep. This is because children are constantly exploring, discovering new things, and generally bettering themselves. We adults get tired too, but it's often not from bettering ourselves. Improving oneself should be a daily commitment. Starting today, what can you do to better yourself?

*'For the best return on your money, pour your purse into your head.'*
– BENJAMIN FRANKLIN

# 45. Mirror, mirror on the wall

Children love pulling faces in front of the mirror. However, as we age, we don't have the same enthusiasm for our reflection. Adults often see themselves more negatively than others see them. Practise looking in the mirror like a child and see your reflection without judgement. Learn to love yourself as you are.

*'Do you want to meet the love of your life?*
*Look in the mirror.'*
– BYRON KATIE

# 46. Children and animals know best

It's been said that animals and children are great at spotting fraudulent personalities in adults. Why? One reason is that children and animals don't pay attention to adults' words because they don't have the ability to understand them fully. They have to rely more on body language cues. Practise watching other people's actions more than listening to their words. What do you observe?

*'Your actions speak so loudly
that I cannot hear what you say.'*
– RALPH WALDO EMERSON

# 47. What is your bedtime?

Seventeen hours of sustained wakefulness leads to a decrease in performance equivalent to a blood-alcohol level of 0.05 per cent. Children are made to go to bed early because of the negative impact a lack of sleep has on them. However, adults quickly adapt to sleep deprivation, believing we can still function normally without sleep when clearly we can't. What is your sleep like?

*'Without enough sleep,*
*we all become tall two-year-olds.'*
– JoJo Jensen

# 48. Develop good sleeping habits

Children and adolescents need about 10 hours sleep a night. Adults need about eight, and those over 65 years can function on six. If you're not getting enough sleep then it's like driving a car that doesn't have all cylinders firing. Be like a child and get into the habit of having a regular bedtime routine.

*'We are what we repeatedly do.*
*Excellence, then, is not an act, but a habit.'*
— ARISTOTLE

# 49. Make a stand

Trying to get a child to do something against their will is very difficult. Adults, on the other hand, comply much more readily, especially when worried that standing up for themselves will offend others. As a result we put our own welfare last. Whether it's politely refusing hospitality or saying no to a salesperson, make a small stand today.

*'The most courageous act is still to think for yourself. Aloud.'*
— COCO CHANEL

# 50. Get into some beach graffiti

A game children play at the beach is trying to write their name in the sand before a wave washes it away. Give it a go. Not only is it fun, it also reminds us that nothing in life lasts forever. Buying expensive things to impress won't impress for long, as things lose their value quickly, both financially and emotionally.

'*Show is a poor substitute for inner worth.*'
— AESOP

# 51. Eat ice-cream fast

As a child did you ever eat ice-cream quickly just to get a headache? Ice-cream headaches are caused by nerves in the roof of your mouth contracting. If you push your tongue up against the roof of your mouth, the nerves relax and the headache goes. Often adults don't see the fun in experiencing discomfort, but it's fear of discomfort that keeps comfort zones alive. Go on, eat some ice-cream quickly and ride out the discomfort.

*'There are only two mistakes one can make along the road to truth; not going all the way, and not starting.'*
– BUDDHA

# 52. Laugh long and loud

Laughing releases feel-good endorphins in our bodies to help increase health, and can fight off ageing and disease. Children love to laugh. If a child's movie doesn't make them laugh then it's often regarded as dull. What can you do to have a laugh and feel happy? And if you're not feeling in the mood, it's more reason to do it.

*'You live longer once you realise that any time spent being unhappy is wasted.'*
– RUTH E. RENKL

# 53. What are you like as a liar?

As adults, we teach children that lying is bad and that honesty is the best policy. Yet we cringe when a child says to their grandmother, 'My mum says you're mean.' Adults spend their lives hiding their true selves from others with everything from hair dye to expensive cars bought on credit. If you were to drop your guard, who would the real you be?

*'Everyone knows a fool when they see one, but not when we are one.'*
— AUTHOR UNKNOWN

# 54. Treat the news with caution

After seeing the September 11 news footage, many children developed fears of planes falling out the sky. Don't be fooled: the news impacts adults too. Fear sells because we're hardwired to place more importance on potential danger than possible gain. Next time you hear bad news, pause before letting the caveman part of your brain believe the doom and gloom. Question everything.

*'If you believe everything you read, better not read.'*

— JAPANESE PROVERB

# 55. Dream to a deadline

When children want something, they want it now. They'll do whatever it takes to get their desired thing. Instead, we adults like to dream about our wants, but we rarely act. Be like a child, go after what you want and set a deadline to get it by.

*'The difference between a goal and a dream is a deadline.'*
— STEVE SMITH

# 56. Fail to succeed

Children don't quit after a failed first attempt – just look at how they learn to walk. However, most adults fear stepping out of their comfort zones in life, especially if the first attempt wasn't successful. Keep the childhood gift alive of not being hindered by fear of failure. Your confidence will soar.

*'I've missed more than 9000 shots in my career. I've lost almost 300 games. Twenty-six times, I've been trusted to take the game winning shot and missed. I've failed over and over and over again in my life. And that is why I succeed.'*
*– Michael Jordan*

# 57. Be a loser

If something is no longer of use to a child then they'll lose it. From half-eaten food to toys they think they've outgrown, children dump the non-essentials. Walk around your home and get rid of things you no longer use. It's freeing to have less.

*'It's not the daily increase but daily decrease. Hack away at the unessential.'*
— BRUCE LEE

# 58. Mess up a cupcake

Children love decorating cupcakes even though they often mess it up. Maybe this is the secret? Try this challenge: decorate a cupcake using your non-dominant hand. You'll feel terribly uncoordinated and will likely make a mess, but it will bring a smile to your face. Go on, learn to laugh at yourself.

*'Move out of your comfort zone. You can only grow if you are willing to feel awkward and uncomfortable when you try something new.'*
— BRIAN TRACY

# 59. Simon says ...

Need to exercise but can't find the
motivation? Approach it like a child. Children
love running, jumping and exploring because
they're having fun. Take out the fun factor
and they wouldn't exercise. Adults often
see exercise as a chore and ignore the fun
side. Simon says, go for a walk and explore
somewhere you haven't been before.

*'An hour of basketball feels like 15 minutes.*
*An hour on a treadmill feels like*
*a weekend in traffic school.'*
— DAVID WALTERS

# 60. Show and tell

As a child did you enjoy showing off your new toys or skills to others? Children don't just talk about their new discovery, they show it in action too. Children learn largely by observing and copying behaviour. Adults are more inclined to tell people what to do. If you want someone to act a certain way, lead by example and show them.

*'Example is not the main thing in influencing others, it is the only thing.'*
– ALBERT SCHWEITZER

# 61. Gamble on your education

Adults like to gamble on things, but they often won't gamble on themselves. Children gamble too, but on themselves instead of on things. A child who is learning to ride a bike is gambling on themselves that they'll be able to learn. What gamble can you take on your self-development and learning?

*'Education is the most powerful weapon which you can use to change the world.'*
– NELSON MANDELA

# 62. Offend people

As adults, our greatest fear, more than dying, is being rejected by others. Children are not yet ruled by this fear and will say what they want instead of what they think people want to hear. Worried you'll offend by saying no? A moment of discomfort by saying no in the present can prevent the future discomfort that would arise from saying yes.

*'It's better to offend someone by saying no, than to fight someone because you said yes.'*
— NEIL JENMAN

# 63. Be read to

Children love being read to by adults. Rekindle your inner child and have adults read to you by listening to audio books on the way to work or while working around the home. It's a simple way to increase your education.

'Give me a man or woman who has read a thousand books and you give me an interesting companion. Give me a man or woman who has read perhaps three and you give me a dangerous enemy indeed.'
– ANNE RICE

# 64. Smile with your eyes

Children are terrible at pretending to look happy. Look back through your family photos at yourself as a child and pick when you're putting on a fake smile. You'll notice that a fake smile doesn't involve the outsides of the eyes wrinkling. How genuine are your smiles these days?

*'If you smile make certain to involve your eyes.'*
— AUTHOR UNKNOWN

# 65. What were your childhood dreams?

What things have you wanted to do since you were little? Every time you hear yourself say 'one day I'm going to…', take note. A life full of regrets is painful. Beginning today what can you do to start ticking off your childhood list of dreams?

*'There is no greater agony than bearing an untold story inside you.'*
– MAYA ANGELOU

# 66. Climb trees

The fear of heights develops at about nine months of age – the same time a child starts crawling. This is for their protection. However, children still love climbing trees, which means mastering this innate fear. If it's not mastered in childhood, the fear of heights can escalate in adulthood. What fears do you need to conquer?

> *'Avoiding danger is no safer in the long run than outright exposure. Life is either a daring adventure, or nothing.'*
> – HELEN KELLER

# 67. Skip when down

Feeling negative about life? Awaken your inner child and skip a short distance (even better, do it in public). It's guaranteed to put a smile on your face.

*'If you've lost your enthusiasm, there's no better place to find it than on a skipping excursion. And, you might just find your lost youth as well!'*
— Jessi Lane Adams

# 68. Play 'chasey' with security

When a child is playing chasey they'll often bait the person who's 'in' by standing inches away from 'home', and then grab home at the last moment to avoid being tagged. Having security close by builds confidence. Whether it's a smoke alarm in your home, being in a stable relationship or having insurance, look for areas where you can increase security in your life, and watch your confidence build.

*'When the mouse laughs at the cat there is a hole nearby.'*
— NIGERIAN PROVERB

# 69. Write down your memories

The part of the brain responsible for memory starts developing at around three years of age. This is why we can't remember our early childhood. A young child's memory is rarely accurate for this reason. Research has shown, however, that adult memory isn't all that reliable either. So don't trust your memory to store all your experiences; write them down.

*'There are some things one remembers even though they may never have happened.'*
– HAROLD PINTER

# 70. Listen in order to persuade

Unlike the eyes, which are almost adult size from birth, the ears never stop growing. Maybe this is why children aren't very good at listening. Does the ability to listen come with age as our ears grow? Unfortunately not. Listening is a rare skill, but it can be developed. Listen to others to increase your influence.

*'The best way to persuade people is with your ears – by listening to them.'*
– DEAN RUSK

# 71. We learn young, but ... we can re-learn as adults

*Children Learn What They Live*

If children live with criticism, they learn to condemn.

If children live with hostility, they learn to fight.

If children live with fear, they learn to be apprehensive.

If children live with pity, they learn to feel sorry for themselves.

If children live with ridicule, they learn to feel shy.

If children live with jealousy, they learn to feel envy.

If children live with shame, they learn to feel guilty.

If children live with encouragement, they learn confidence.

If children live with tolerance, they learn patience.
If children live with praise, they learn appreciation.
If children live with acceptance, they learn to love.
If children live with approval, they learn to like
themselves.
If children live with recognition, they learn it is
good to have a goal.
If children live with sharing, they learn generosity.
If children live with honesty, they learn truthfulness.
If children live with fairness, they learn justice.
If children live with kindness and consideration,
they learn respect.
If children live with security, they learn to have
faith in themselves and in those about them.
If children live with friendliness, they learn the
world is a nice place in which to live.

— DOROTHY LAW NOLTE

# 72. Break the fast with breakfast

Schools now encourage children to have breakfast before starting school, as an empty stomach prevents them from working and learning well. Yet many of us still think we can skip breakfast and continue to function normally. Try driving your car on an empty tank of fuel and see how far you get. What did you have for brekkie today?

*'One should not attend even the end of the world without a good breakfast.'*
– ROBERT A. HEINLEIN

# 73. Breathe like a child

We all breathe. Babies and children do it properly, though very few adults do – the older we get, the more shallowly we inhale. The stress of everyday life makes adults breathe incorrectly. Try taking up yoga to learn about breathing. Until then, concentrate on slowing down your breathing and taking in deep breaths. It'll give you a natural advantage and increase your wellbeing.

*'When you own your breath,*
*nobody can steal your peace.'*
– Author unknown

# 74. Invite friends over

Children are obsessed with having friends over to play, regardless of what state the house is in. Many adults refrain from inviting friends over due to feeling judged about their home. Renting, small house, dirty house, unfinished gardens – put all these aside and trust that true friends will accept you just as you are. We need friends in our lives. Starting today, organise to have a friend over.

*'It is more shameful to distrust our friends than to be deceived by them.'*
– CONFUCIUS

# 75. Unlearn deception

Adults often tell white lies to children with the belief it's for the child's own good. It's likely you've learned deception from a young age and now use it as an adult. The question is, will you keep using white lies now that it's been brought to your attention?

*'Adults find pleasure in deceiving a child. They consider it necessary, but they also enjoy it. The children very quickly figure it out and then practise deception themselves.'*
— ELIAS CANETTI

# 76. Fly a kite

A great joy for children is flying a kite. Try it as an adult. It's cheap, relaxing and frees your mind because it requires a strong focus on reading nature.

*'You will find truth more quickly*
*through delight than gravity.*
*Let out a little more string on your kite.'*
— ALAN COHEN

# 77. Follow with caution

Humans are a herd animal: we naturally follow. Yet children seem to do this less than adults. They'll act themselves, wear mismatching clothes and take pride in doing things uniquely. If you can resist the pull of the herd, success will come much easier and be more satisfying. Be like a child and act in ways that are true to yourself.

*'Whenever you find yourself on the side of the majority, it is time to pause and reflect.'*
— Mark Twain

# 78. Know your stereotypes

Both boys and girls in 1600s England and New England wore dresses until they were about seven years old. Likewise, up until the 1930s the colour pink was for boys, and blue for girls. What stereotypes are you living by? And what can you do to break them?

*'People are incapable of stereotyping you; you stereotype yourself because you're the one who accepts roles that put you in this rut or in this stereotype.'*
— EVA MENDES

# 79. Try incidental exercise

Incidental exercise is the exercise you
get when exercising isn't your primary
motivation. We're talking vacuuming or
mopping floors, walking to the shop,
taking the stairs or working in your garden.
Research has found this is the secret to fit,
healthy children. Don't have time to exercise?
Then learn from a child and incorporate it
into your everyday life.

*'Those who think they have not time for
bodily exercise will sooner or later have
to find time for illness.'*
— EDWARD STANLEY

# 80. Role-play

Interestingly, children will experiment by pretending to be different people. This creative process aids personality development. Go someplace where no-one knows you and act like you're someone else. It's scary, but freeing.

> *'The best way of successfully*
> *acting a part is to be it.'*
> – ARTHUR CONAN DOYLE

# 81. Keep ambitions child-friendly

Ask a child what they want to achieve and they'll tell you in simple terms. Sometimes we give in to procrastination because following our goals has become too complex. You don't have to dumb your goals down, just make them more straightforward. In a few words, write down what you want to achieve.

*'If you can't explain it to a six-year-old, you don't understand it yourself.'*
– ALBERT EINSTEIN

# 82. Are you addicted to stress?

Do you lead a very stressful life? Research shows you'll be more inclined to keep it that way, even if it doesn't need to be, because your body becomes addicted to stress hormones. Children won't tolerate stressful activities like adults and will simply refuse to partake in them. How many responsibilities in your life are by choice or habit rather than necessity?

*'Every form of addiction is bad,*
*no matter whether the narcotic be*
*alcohol or morphine or idealism.'*
— CARL GUSTAV JUNG

# 83. Stress-addiction checklist

The following signs may indicate that stress is an issue in your life:

1. Chronic lack of ability to focus
2. Overwhelming desire to maintain routine
3. Habitual procrastination
4. Overall lethargy
5. Persistent negativity.

If you've ticked all five, it could be time to acknowledge the problem and start making changes in your life. Maybe consider seeing a health professional.

*'You do anything long enough to escape the habit of living until the escape becomes the habit.'*
– DAVID RYAN

# 84. Surprise yourself

Children love being surprised. Why?
Being surprised shakes us out of traditional
thinking and opens the mind to new
possibilities. Try doing new and unusual
things or going places you wouldn't normally.
See what impact the unexpected has on you,
especially if you do things that prove long-
held beliefs about yourself wrong.

*'It doesn't take much to surprise others, but to
surprise oneself – now that is a great feat.'*
– KRISTEN HARTLEY

# 85. The fear of emotion

Anger, sadness, excitement and joy are just some of the emotions children display regularly. As adults, we generally prefer to bottle our emotions. The problem is that unexpressed emotions have been linked to depression, heart disease and even cancer. Expressing emotions isn't as scary as the risks associated with not expressing them.

*'Emotion will not drive you crazy. What will drive you crazy is the fear of emotion.'*
— Author unknown

# 86. What's your food additive?

Why is it that children aren't allowed to have too much of a good thing, such as chocolate, screen time, sugar or food additives, but as adults our addictions are seen as necessities? Whether it's shopping, food, cigarettes, or the internet, generally we all have an addiction of some sort. What's yours? Break it before it breaks you.

*'This left me alone to solve the coffee problem – a sort of catch-22, as in order to think straight I need caffeine, and in order to make that happen I need to think straight.'*
– DAVID SEDARIS

# 87. Resist comfort eating

We all comfort eat to some degree when stressed. One reason we eat junk is because our bodies are craving high-energy sugary or fatty foods to *maintain* our stressed state. The problem with junk food is the 'high' is followed quickly by a downer. Tantrums often pass quicker for children who aren't allowed junk food. Next time you have cravings, keep busy; your internal tantrum will pass.

*'Food is the most primitive form of comfort.'*
– SHEILAH GRAHAM

# 88. Know the meaning of your words

My son, at age two, said, 'I hurt my tentacles!' when he slipped with his legs either side of the edge of the bath. Adults, too, can often fail to fully understand the true meaning of the words we express out of habit. Words such as 'should', 'try', 'might', 'but', 'can't' and 'someday' all help sow failure in your subconscious. Beware of what you are telling yourself.

*'The inner speech, your thoughts, can cause you to be rich or poor, loved or unloved, happy or unhappy, attractive or unattractive, powerful or weak.'*
– RALPH CHARELL

# 89. You can't escape your tongue print

Just like your fingerprints, your 'tongue print' is unique to you. Trying to act or talk like someone else is risky because not only can you be seen as copying, but it robs you of your uniqueness. True achievement in life is being able to be yourself.

*'Be who you are and say what you feel*
*because those who mind don't matter*
*and those who matter don't mind.'*
— Dr. Seuss

# 90. Dare to dream

When it comes to dreams and ambitions, children will believe virtually anything is possible. Adults tend to go the other way completely as a form of self-protection against failure. This is why most people will kindly tell you why pursuing your dream won't work – they think they're protecting you. There's only one problem: it's *your* dream they're dashing.

> *'At first dreams seem impossible, then improbable, then inevitable.'*
> – CHRISTOPHER REEVE

# 91. Make time to waste time

Our society is so time-obsessed that often doing anything other than work is seen as wasting time, which triggers guilt. When we see children wasting time it can even make us agitated. Get around this negative feeling by designating time to do nothing. Children are experts at wasting time, or are they really wasting time? Try it and see.

*'Time you enjoy wasting is not wasted time.'*
— MARTHE TROLY-CURTIN

# 92. Play dress-ups

Children love to get dressed up in clothes they wouldn't normally wear. Added to that, a child will often change their personality to suit the dress-ups they have on. Without going to extremes, be daring and wear something out in public you wouldn't normally. How are your clothes controlling you?

*'People dress how they feel.'*
— AUTHOR UNKNOWN

# 93. Moderation is key

Research shows that children are good at listening to their bodies. Too much screen time and they'll want exercise, or too much junk food and they'll want healthy food. Find balance in your life by listening to your body. It will tell you when the things you are doing to yourself are out of balance and you need a change.

*'Use, do not abuse; neither abstinence nor excess ever renders man happy.'*
— VOLTAIRE

# 94. Wait and you'll see

Research shows that if a child is taught to wait or save up for something they want instead of getting it straight away they're likely to be happier in life. Psychologists call this delayed gratification. Before you next use your credit card, pause. Is this something you can save up for instead? Delayed gratification will bring you far more reward than any purchase ever can.

*'True happiness ... is not attained through self-gratification, but through fidelity to a worthy purpose.'*
– HELEN KELLER

# 95. Jigsaw-puzzle your life

Do you remember doing jigsaw puzzles as a child? It's likely you would have first turned all the pieces over right way up, then sorted them into groups according to colour. Patiently picking away at it made the picture come to life. Treat your adult life the same way. Break things down into manageable tasks instead of focusing on the final outcome and you'll see your life come together.

*'Nothing is particularly hard*
*if you divide it into small jobs.'*
– HENRY FORD

# 96. Don't worry about worry

Whether it's monsters under the bed or the sky falling in, children's worries are often humorous to adults. But it's human nature to predict the worst; trouble is, we're lousy at it. Keep a diary of how often you're right after anticipating the worst possible outcome. How accurate do you think your predictions are going to be?

*'If you want to test your memory,*
*try to recall what you were worrying*
*about one year ago today.'*
– E. JOSEPH COSSMAN

# 97. Practise sleep writing

The mind goes over and over things because it fears we will forget them before we've reached a resolution. Keep a note pad by your bed and if you have any worries in the night, write them down. You'll sleep better for it.

*'I put a piece of paper under my pillow,*
*and when I could not sleep*
*I wrote in the dark.'*
— HENRY DAVID THOREAU

# 98. Eat chocolate

It's a no-brainer that if you want a protesting child to do something they don't want to do, you offer them chocolate. Rewarded behaviour gets repeated – and this is true throughout our lives. Do the thing you've been putting off, and once done, reward yourself with chocolate or something else that you like. You'll be surprised how much more likely you'll be to go back and do it again.

*'Once in a while I say, "Go for it"*
*and I eat chocolate.'*
– CLAUDIA SCHIFFER

# 99. Give your courage a work-out

We encourage children to face their fears and we praise them when they do. Why? Because the quality of a person's life depends on how they react to the fears they face. Want to improve your life? Then take a risk and exercise your courage.

> *'Life shrinks or expands in proportion to one's courage.'*
> – ANAÏS NIN

# 100. Watch a children's movie

When a child watches a movie they become totally engrossed by it, while as adults we prefer to pick a movie to pieces, questioning everything. Challenge yourself and watch a children's movie, imagining you're watching it as a child. That means everything is believable. Just enjoy the experience without passing judgement.

*'I have a theory that movies operate on the level of dreams, where you dream yourself.'*
— MERYL STREEP

# 101. Own your bed

Children aren't worried about making their bed each morning. Many adults can't leave the house until their own bed is made. Children own their beds but many adults find that their bed owns them. What objects are you letting control you?

*'No one ever died from sleeping*
*in an unmade bed.'*
— ERMA BOMBECK

# 102. Take some body pride

'Look how tall/strong I am!'
'Watch me stand on one foot.'
Children take pride in their bodies.
Interestingly, the more adults care for their
bodies, the more pride they take in theirs,
too. Forget those same-old excuses about
being too busy with work to take care of
yourself. What can you do to look after your
body? It's the only one you've got.

*'No one on their deathbed ever wished*
*they'd spent more time at work.'*
— AUTHOR UNKNOWN

# 103. Share your talent

Children are often encouraged by adults to share. Yet adults don't always take their own advice, especially when it comes to sharing talents. We all have a talent that the world can benefit from. It takes courage, but how can you help share your talent? It's often the small acts that have the biggest impact.

*'If you are planning for a year, sow rice; if you are planning for a decade, plant trees; if you are planning for a lifetime, educate people.'*
— CHINESE PROVERB

# 104. Look where you want to go

Children learning gymnastics are taught that if they look toward the direction they want to go, their bodies will follow. Success in any field is similar. Focus on where you want to go in life and success will follow.

*'Don't look back, you're not going that way.'*
— Author unknown

# 105. Let go of your security blanket

We see children's security blankets as things they will (and should) soon grow out of. However, many adults have security blankets of their own. We stay in comfort zones that make us feel safe – unrewarding jobs, unhappy relationships – and avoid taking risks. Even though they're unrewarding, comfort zones, like security blankets, feel temporarily good. But these feelings inevitably wear off. Instead of trying to get rid of immediate discomfort, put your energies into achieving a goal.

*'Failures do what is tension relieving, while winners do what is goal achieving.'*
– DENIS WAITLEY

# 106. We are all dying

Death and taxes are the only certainties in life. While children don't pay taxes, they're often fascinated by death. However, many adults spend so much of their lives pretending death doesn't exist that they miss out on truly living. Psychologists have shown that people who can embrace this instead of running from it have far happier and richer lives. Be like a child and make yourself consciously aware of your own mortality by surrounding yourself with physical reminders. If this sounds strange, it's because you're thinking like an adult and not a child.

*'This is your life and it's ending one minute at a time.'*
– BRAD PITT AS TYLER DURDEN IN *FIGHT CLUB*

# 107. Everything has value

A wise old monk holds up a handful of mud
to the student and asks which is more useful:
a piece of gold or a pile of mud? The student
replies, 'The gold of course.' To which the
wise monk says, 'but to a seed?' Children are
good at placing value on things that don't
cost money. Adults often find it harder to
see the immediate value of many things that
don't have a price tag. How valuable are
your relationships, family, health and work in
helping you live a meaningful life?

*'Price is what you pay.*
*Value is what you get.'*
– WARREN BUFFETT

# 108. Work with the hand you were dealt

Life can be cruel and deal us a hand that isn't fair. But whether you face hardships in the areas of health, education, wealth or family, focusing solely on the negatives won't change anything. Children with physical setbacks still live life to the fullest, finding enjoyment in the things they *can* do. How can you turn your perceived weakness into a strength?

*'Life is like a game of cards. The hand that is dealt you represents determinism; the way you play it is free will.'*
— JAWAHARLAL NEHRU

# 109. Like attracts like

A young child who is excited will quickly excite a whole group of their peers. The people you associate with will play a large role in influencing how you lead your life. Be honest with yourself and ask: what influence are the people in your life having on you?

*'By associating with wise people you will become wise yourself.'*
— MENANDER

# 110. Avoid the blame game

Children are discouraged from blaming others when things don't go their way. Instead they're encouraged to take responsibility for the consequences of their own actions. However, just like children, adults often also blame others when things don't go our way. Blaming others takes away our control. Being grateful for the positives in life gives it back.

*'Do not blame God for having created the tiger, but thank him for not having given it wings.'*
— INDIAN PROVERB

# 111. See your future

Children are often planning what they want to be when they're older. Planning for your future may seem like boring work that takes you away from enjoying yourself right now. However, delaying gratification will pay rich rewards in the future.

*'It wasn't raining when Noah built the Ark.'*
— HOWARD RUFF

# 112. Five steps to greatness

Children like following a process – albeit not always someone else's process. There's a way to butter toast, a formula for colouring-in and a system for playing games. As adults, there's a formula for success in life, and it involves knowing your own process and sticking to it.

> *'The first step in the acquisition*
> *of wisdom is silence,*
> *The second listening,*
> *The third memory,*
> *The fourth practice,*
> *The fifth teaching others.'*
> – SOLOMON IBN GABIROL

# 113. Treat friends like assets

Children want to have lots of friends. Good friendships have been linked with increased health and life expectancy. The problem is adults often take close friends for granted. Starting today, make contact with that close friend you've been meaning to contact, but haven't.

> *'Friends are lost by calling too often
> and calling too seldom.'*
> — FRENCH PROVERB

# 114. Hold grudges like a child

Any trip to the playground will show you that children are quick to fall out with each other, but equally swift at forgetting their grudges, making up and getting back to business. Yet adults can hold grudges that last for years. Holding a grudge can have negative impacts on our health and has been causally linked to heart disease, depression and even cancer. What grudge are you holding onto?

*'Not forgiving is like drinking rat poison and then waiting for the rat to die.'*
– ANNE LAMOTT

# 115. Who is your job turning you into?

When children play-act being grown-ups, their personality will change to suit the profession they're acting out. Make no mistake: your job is changing you. If it's a job you enjoy then the change will likely be positive and empowering. However, if you don't like your job, it will be chipping away at your happiness and self-respect. Consider making steps to change. Your personality depends on it.

*'You know you are on the road to success if you would do your job and not be paid for it.'*
– OPRAH WINFREY

# 116. Get outdoors

School teachers working with young children often dread rainy days. Children love the outdoors and can go a little wild if they can't get out and about. Let your inner child be free. Step outside, preferably with nature, and notice the impact it has on you.

*'Look deep into nature, and then you will understand everything better.'*
— ALBERT EINSTEIN

# 117. Respect others' faults

Children can be completely oblivious to adults' faults. Yet we will often see the faults in others that we may subconsciously recognise in ourselves. Next time you become annoyed by what someone has done, look within and ask yourself, 'How does this fault apply to me?'

> *'Deal with the faults of others*
> *as gently as with your own.'*
> – CHINESE PROVERB

# 118. Time-poor excuses are poor

We're all familiar with the old saying that if you want something done quickly, ask a busy person to do it. The secret to time management is prioritising what's most important in life. Children are great at putting their most important needs, desires and activities first. Does trying to impress others come before or after your own needs?

*'Don't say you don't have enough time.*
*You have exactly the same number of hours*
*per day that were given to Helen Keller, Pasteur,*
*Michelangelo, Mother Teresa, Leonardo da Vinci,*
*Thomas Jefferson and Albert Einstein.'*
*– H. Jackson Brown, Jr*

# 119. Get a life

Both children and adults dream of being successful and famous. However, these dreams and ambitions don't rule a child's life. If fame and success are all you want, then your existence will be pretty empty. You need a life outside of your dream, otherwise it can warp the soul. Be vigilant.

*'Here's a tip to avoid "death by celebrity": First off, get a life. They can't touch you if you're out doing something interesting.'*
– Kent Nichols and Douglas Sarine

# 120. Talk with passion about your passion

Nothing is more infectious than listening to a child who is passionate about something. What are you passionate about? It takes courage to share your passion, but it gets easier with each go.

*'When I hear a man preach, I like to see him act as if he were fighting bees.'*
— ABRAHAM LINCOLN

# 121. If at first you succeed, try, try again

Children will strive to reach personal goals like learning to ride a bike. But once conquered, they're onto their next challenge. Reaching a goal is exciting. Stopping after reaching it is fatal. Once you've taken the time to acknowledge your achievement, attaining a goal should be merely the motivation to set new and bigger goals. Quitting due to success is more dangerous than quitting due to failure.

*'If you have accomplished all that you planned*
*for yourself, you have not planned enough.'*
— EDWARD EVERETT HALE

# 122. Find balance

When children are tired, they rest; when hungry, they eat; when motivated they play. Find balance in your life. Listen to your body because it will tell you when the things you are doing to yourself are out of balance.

*'To put everything in balance is good,*
*to put everything in harmony is better.'*
— VICTOR HUGO

# 123. Who are you entrusting your life to?

When a child has a new idea, others' negative comments often won't deter them. However, we adults are very receptive to others' negative advice, which can stop our dreams instantly. It's okay to get advice from others. However, it's your choice whether you want to entrust your life to their opinions.

*'When you go into court you are putting your fate into the hands of twelve people who weren't smart enough to get out of jury duty.'*
— NORM CROSBY

# 124. Swing high

As you follow your dreams you will have down days and moments when you question yourself. On days like these, listen to your inner child and go outside and play. Even better, try out the playground swings: swing high and your mood will follow.

*'My father would take me to the playground, and put me on mood swings.'*
— JAY LONDON

# Acknowledgements

Jonathan Dyer, thanks for helping me create
this book; Mel, my wife and best friend, and
my children, Emma and Patrick; my agent
Sally Bird; Fran Berry and the team from
Hardie Grant Books, for giving me another
opportunity; my editor Helen Withycombe, for
taking this book to a whole new level; my PhD
supervisors Associate Professor Ross Menzies,
Dr Sue O'Brian, Professor Mark Onslow
and Associate Professor Ann Packman at the
University of Sydney's Australian Stuttering
Research Centre; my parents Ron and Helen;
my parents-in-law Bruce and Cynthya; my
big brother Mick and his family Leanne, Ben,
Jade and Mitchell; my brother Ian and his

wife Nikki; my sister Kazz and her husband Adrian; my nephew Zack and niece Ivy; my grandmother Marie Thorold; David Thorold, my 'Uncle D' in New Guinea, his wife Sal and their daughter Sophia; my cousins Mary-Anne, Ron, Ollie and her husband Jude, and their kids Tonna and Malia; my uncle Ron and aunt Dee; Aunty Anne, who is in our hearts forever; and my uncle Neil, and Brent and Sarah.

# About the author

Psychologist and anxiety specialist Anthony
Gunn has developed a reputation for helping
people step out of their comfort zones.
Anthony became a psychologist for selfish
reasons; he wanted to treat himself for a phobia
of medical procedures after undergoing an
emergency operation for a collapsed lung –
without anaesthetic – and was hospitalised
for three months while on a student exchange
program in Honduras, Central America.
Anthony's publications include *Walk Tall:
100 Ways to Live Life to the Fullest* and *Raising
Confident Happy Children: 40 tips for helping
your child succeed.*

For more info go to: www.anthonygunn.com

Published in 2013 by Hardie Grant Books

Hardie Grant Books (Australia)
Ground Floor, Building 1
658 Church Street
Richmond, Victoria 3121
www.hardiegrant.com.au

Hardie Grant Books (UK)
Dudley House, North Suite
34–35 Southampton Street
London WC2E 7HF
www.hardiegrant.co.uk

pp. 76–77 excerpted from the book CHILDREN LEARN WHAT
THEY LIVE
Copyright © 1998 by Dorothy Law Nolte and Rachel Harris
The poem "Children Learn What They Live"
Copyright ©1972 by Dorothy Law Nolte
Used by permission of Workman Publishing Co., Inc., New York
All Rights Reserved

A Cataloguing-in-Publication entry is available from the catalogue
of the National Library of Australia at www.nla.gov.au
Swing High: Life lessons from childhood
ISBN 978 1 74270 595 8

Cover design by LANZ+MARTIN
Typeset in Plantin Light 11/17pt by Cannon Typesetting
Colour reproduction by Splitting Image Colour Studio
Printed and bound in China by 1010 Printing International Limited